For
My Best Friend
Marja

ON
Friendship
A SELECTION

Edited by

LOUISE BACHELDER

PETER PAUPER PRESS, INC.
WHITE PLAINS • NEW YORK

*I love you not only for what you are,
but for what I am when I am with you.*

*I love you not only for what you have
made of yourself, but for what you are
making of me.*

*I love you because you have done more
than any creed could have done to make
me good, and more than any fate could
have done to make me happy.*

*You have done it without a touch, with-
out a word, without a sign.*

*You have done it by being yourself. Per-
haps that is what being a friend means,
after all.*

ANONYMOUS

On Friendship

BE COURTEOUS to all, but intimate with few; and let those few be well tried before you give them your confidence. True friendship is a plant of slow growth, and must undergo and withstand the shocks of adversity before it is entitled to the appellation.

GEORGE WASHINGTON

Don't flatter yourself that friendship authorizes you to say disagreeable things to your intimates. The nearer you come into relation with a person, the more necessary do tact and courtesy become. Except in cases of necessity, which are rare, leave your friend to learn unpleasant things from his enemies; they are ready enough to tell them.

OLIVER WENDELL HOLMES

So LONG as we love, we serve. So long as we are loved by others, I would almost say we are indispensable; and no man is useless while he has a friend.   ROBERT LOUIS STEVENSON

Friend is a word of Royal tone
Friend is a Poem all alone.
                              A PERSIAN POET

SENTIMENTS are what unites people, opinions what separates them. Sentiments are a simple bond that gathers us together; opinions represent the principle of variety that scatters. The friendships of youth are founded on the former, the cliques of old age are to be blamed on the latter. If we could only realize this early and arrive at a liberal view as regards others in cultivating our own attitude of mind, we would be more conciliatory and try to collect by the bond of sentiment what opinion has dispersed.

JOHANN WOLFGANG VON GOETHE

THE right course is to choose for a friend one who is frank, sociable and sympathetic — that is, one who is likely to be influenced by the same motives as yourself — since all these qualities induce to loyalty. . . . Since happiness is our best and highest aim we must, if we would attain it, give our attention to virtue, without which we can obtain neither friendship nor any other desirable thing.

MARCUS TULLIUS CICERO

———————————

BE SLOW in choosing a friend, slower in changing. BENJAMIN FRANKLIN

———————————

. . . I HAVE never made an acquaintance since that lasted, or a friendship that answered with any that had not some tincture of the absurd in their characters. . . . I venerate an honest obligation of understanding. The more laughable blunders a man shall commit in your company, the more tests he giveth you that he will not betray or overreach you.

CHARLES LAMB

A BOOK is a friend; a good book is a good friend. It will talk to you when you want it to talk, and it will keep still when you want it to keep still — and there are not many friends who know enough to do that. A library is a collection of friends.   LYMAN ABBOTT

———————

You mention that you *feel yourself hurt.* Permit me to offer you a maxim, which has thro' life been of use to me and may be so to you in preventing imaginary hurts. It is, always to *suppose* one's friends *may be right* till one *finds* them wrong; rather than to *suppose them wrong* till one finds them right. You have heard and imagined all that can be said or suppos'd on one side of the question, but not on the other.   BENJAMIN FRANKLIN

———————

FRIENDSHIPS last when each friend thinks he has a slight superiority over the other.
                    HONORÉ DE BALZAC

THE making of friends, who are real friends, is the best token we have of a man's success in life. EDWARD EVERETT HALE

WHO ceases to be a friend, never was one.

ANONYMOUS

TWO MAY talk and one may hear, but three cannot take part in a conversation of the most sincere and searching sort.

RALPH WALDO EMERSON

THE most I can do for my friend is simply to be his friend. I have no wealth to bestow on him. If he knows that I am happy in loving him, he will want no other reward. Is not friendship divine in this?

HENRY DAVID THOREAU

A FRIEND to all is a friend to none.

ARISTOTLE

THE end of friendship is a commerce the most strict and homely that can be joined; more strict than any of which we have experience. It is for aid and comfort through all the relations and passages of life and death. It is fit for serene days, and graceful gifts, and country rambles, but also for rough roads and hard fare, shipwreck, poverty, and persecution. It keeps company with the sallies of the wit and the trances of religion. We are to dignify to each other the daily needs and offices of man's life, and embellish it by courage, wisdom and unity. It should never fall into something usual and settled, but should be alert and inventive, and add rhyme and reason to what was drudgery.

RALPH WALDO EMERSON

———————◆———————

FRIENDSHIP that flows from the heart cannot be frozen by adversity, as the water that flows from the spring cannot congeal in winter.   JAMES FENIMORE COOPER

ONE friend in a lifetime is much; two are many; three are hardly possible. Friendship needs a certain parallelism of life, a community of thought, a rivalry of aim. . . . Friends are born, not made. . . . Intimates are predestined. HENRY BROOKS ADAMS

———◆———

THE holy passion of Friendship is of so sweet and steady and loyal and enduring a nature that it will last through a whole lifetime, if not asked to lend money.

SAMUEL L. CLEMENS

———◆———

EVERY man should have a fair sized cemetery in which to bury the faults of his friends.

HENRY BROOKS ADAMS

———◆———

BE NOT the fourth friend of him who had three before and lost them.

JOHN CASPER LAVATER

I DO not wish to treat friendships daintily, but with roughest courage. When they are real, they are not glass threads or frost-work, but the solidest thing we know.

RALPH WALDO EMERSON

———◆———

TRUE happiness consists not in the multitude of friends, but in their worth and choice.

BEN JONSON

———◆———

FRIENDSHIP renders prosperity more brilliant, while it lightens adversity by sharing it and making its burden common.

MARCUS TULLIUS CICERO

———◆———

"STAY" is a charming word in a friend's vocabulary.   AMOS BRONSON ALCOTT

———◆———

SOMETHING like home that is not home is to be desired; it is found in the house of a friend.

SIR WILLIAM TEMPLE

BLESSED are they who have the gift of making friends, for it is one of God's best gifts. It involves many things, but above all, the power of going out of one's self, and appreciating whatever is noble and loving in another.   THOMAS HUGHES

A FRIEND is a person with whom I may be sincere. Before him, I may think aloud.

RALPH WALDO EMERSON

FRIENDSHIP is the only thing in the world concerning the usefulness of which all mankind are agreed.   MARCUS TULLIUS CICERO

A MAN's friendships are one of the best measures of his worth.   CHARLES DARWIN

PURE friendship is something which men of an inferior intellect can never taste.

JEAN DE LA BRUYÈRE

THERE are many moments in friendship, as in love, when silence is beyond words. The faults of our friend may be clear to us, but it is well to seem to shut our eyes to them.

Friendship is usually treated by the majority of mankind as a tough and everlasting thing which will survive all manner of bad treatment. But this is an exceedingly great and foolish error; it may die in an hour of a single unwise word. . . .

MARIE LOUISE DE LA RAMÉE *(Ouida)*

Do NOT save your loving speeches
For your friends till they are dead;
Do not write them on their tombstones,
Speak them rather now instead.

ANNA CUMMINS

FRIENDSHIP is a word the very sight of which in print makes the heart warm.

AUGUSTINE BIRRELL

A SLENDER acquaintance with the world must convince every man that actions, not words, are the true criterion of the attachment of friends; and that the most liberal professions of good-will are very far from being the surest marks of it.   GEORGE WASHINGTON

———◆———

THE method for the culture of friendship finds its best and briefest summary in the Golden Rule.   HUGH BLACK

———◆———

IT IS a good thing to be rich, and a good thing to be strong, but it is a better thing to be beloved of many friends.   EURIPIDES

———◆———

NO DISTANCE of place or lapse of time can lessen the friendship of those who are thoroughly persuaded of each other's worth.

ROBERT SOUTHEY

THEY that love beyond the world can not be separated by it. Death can not kill what never dies.

. . . Nor can spirits ever be divided, that love and live in the same divine principle, the root and record, of their friendship.

. . . Death is but crossing the world as friends do the seas; they live in one another still. . . .

This is the comfort of friends, that though they may be said to die, yet their friendship and society are, in the best sense, ever present because immortal.   WILLIAM PENN

———◆———

AFFECTION can withstand very severe storms of vigor, but not a long polar frost of indifference.   SIR WALTER SCOTT

———◆———

WHEN befriended, remember it,
When you befriend, — forget it.
   BENJAMIN FRANKLIN

IF A man does not make new acquaintances
as he advances through life, he will soon find
himself alone. A man, sir, should keep his
friendships in constant repair.

SAMUEL JOHNSON

FRIENDS? Yes. Not only friends in flesh,
Not merely friends in time and space;
I want these, but I want as well
The friends of all the human race,
As Lincoln, Shakespeare, Jesus — souls
That make the universe their throne,
And yet from that high seat can stoop
And speak with each of us alone.

ST. CLAIR ADAMS

THE only rose without thorns is friendship.

MADELEINE DE SCUDÉRY

WE ARE advertis'd by our loving friends.

WILLIAM SHAKESPEARE

No FRIENDSHIP can survive the gift of gold. The generous can indeed forget that they have given, but the grateful can never forget that they have received.

WILLIAM HENRY SMITH

IN THE life of a young man the most essential thing for happiness is the gift of friendship.

SIR WILLIAM OSLER

IT IS one of the severest tests of friendship to tell your friend his faults. — So to love a man that you cannot bear to see a stain upon him, and to speak painful truth through loving words, that is friendship.

HENRY WARD BEECHER

TRUE friendship's laws are by this rule
     express'd,
Welcome the coming, speed the parting
     guest.   ALEXANDER POPE

THE friends thou hast, and their adoption
    tried,
Grapple them to thy soul with hoops of steel;
But do not dull thy palm with entertainment
Of each new-hatch'd, unfledg'd comrade.
    Beware
Of entrance to a quarrel; but being in,
Bear't that th' opposed may beware of thee.
Give every man thine ear, but few thy voice;
Take each man's censure, but reserve thy
    judgment . . .
Neither a borrower, nor a lender be;
For loan oft loses itself and friend,
And borrowing dulls the edge of husbandry.
This above all: to thine own self be true,
And it must follow, as the night the day,
Thou canst not then be false to any man.

WILLIAM SHAKESPEARE

THE first foundation of friendship is not the
power of conferring benefits but the equal-
ity with which they are received, and may be
returned.   JUNIUS

ARE new friends who are worthy of friendship, to be preferred to old friends? The question is unworthy of a human being, for there should be no surfeit of friendships as there is of other things; and, as in the case of wines that improve with age, the oldest friendships ought to be the most delightful; moreover, the well-known adage is true: "Men must eat many a peck of salt together before the claims of friendship are fulfilled."

MARCUS TULLIUS CICERO

I DO then with my friends as I do with my books. I would have them where I can find them, but I seldom use them.

RALPH WALDO EMERSON

FRIENDSHIP is a thing most necessary to life, since without friends no one would choose to live, though possessed of all other advantages.

ARISTOTLE

THE essence of friendship is entireness, a total magnanimity and trust.

RALPH WALDO EMERSON

THE feeling of friendship is like that of being comfortably filled with roast beef; love, like being enlivened with champagne.

SAMUEL JOHNSON

WHEN true friends meet in adverse hour,
'Tis like a sunbeam through a shower.
A watery way an instant seen,
The darkly closing clouds between.

SIR WALTER SCOTT

NOTHING makes the earth seem so spacious as to have friends at a distance; they make the latitudes and the longitudes.

HENRY DAVID THOREAU

KEEP well thy tongue and keep thy friends.

GEOFFREY CHAUCER

FRIENDSHIP, like love, is destroyed by long absence, though it may be increased by short intermissions.   SAMUEL JOHNSON

———————◆———————

WHEN my friends are one-eyed, I look at their profile.   JOSEPH JOUBERT

———————◆———————

ALONSO OF ARAGON was wont to say in com-
mendation of age that age appears to be best
in four things: old wood best to burn, old
wine to drink, old friends to trust, and old
authors to read.   FRANCIS BACON

———————◆———————

ELYSIUM is as far as to
The very nearest room,
If in that room a friend await
Felicity or doom.

                                        EMILY DICKINSON

———————◆———————

HAPPY is the house that shelters a friend.
                                        RALPH WALDO EMERSON

GREATER love hath no man than this, that a man lay down his life for his friend.

ST. JOHN 15:13

———◆———

A PRINCIPAL fruit of friendship is the ease and discharge of the fullness of the heart, which passions of all kinds do cause and induce. We know diseases of stoppings and suffocations are the most dangerous in the body; and it is not much otherwise in the mind: you may take sarza to open the liver, steel to open the spleen, flower of sulphur for the lungs, castoreum for the brain; but no receipt openeth the heart but a true friend, to whom you may impart griefs, joys, fears, hopes, suspicions, counsels, and whatsoever lieth upon the heart to oppress it, in a kind of civil shrift or confusion. . . .

FRANCIS BACON

———◆———

A FRIEND is a present you give yourself.

ROBERT LOUIS STEVENSON

UNDER the magnetism of friendship the modest man becomes bold; the shy, confident; the lazy, active; or the impetuous, prudent and peaceful.

WILLIAM MAKEPEACE THACKERAY

"I WOULD go up to the gates of hell with a
    friend,
Through thick and thin."
The other said, as he bit off a concha's end,
"I would go in."   JOHN ERNEST McCANN

SMALL service is true service while it lasts;
Of friends however humble, scorn not one;
The daisy, by the shadow that it casts,
Protects the lingering dewdrop from the sun.

WILLIAM WORDSWORTH

THE only reward of virtue is virtue; the only way to have a friend is to be one.

RALPH WALDO EMERSON

To PRESERVE a friend three things are necessary: to honor him present, praise him absent, and assist him in his necessities.

PROVERB FROM THE ITALIAN

A FRIEND is one to whom one may pour out all the contents of one's heart, chaff and grain together, knowing that the gentlest of hands will take and sift it, keep what is worth keeping and with the breath of kindness blow the rest away.

ARABIAN PROVERB

THERE was once a pretty chicken, but
   his friends were pretty few,
For he thought that there was nothing
   in the world but what he knew.

MARION DOUGLAS

LAUGHTER is not a bad beginning for a friendship, and it is the best ending for one.

OSCAR WILDE

THERE is after all something in those trifles
that friends bestow upon each other which
is an unfailing indication of the place the
giver holds in the affections. I would believe
that one who preserved a lock of hair, a
simple flower, or any trifle of my bestowing,
loved me, though no show was made of it;
while all the protestations in the world would
not win my confidence in one who set no
value on such little things.

Trifles they may be; but it is by such that
character and disposition are oftenest re-
vealed.   WASHINGTON IRVING

———————◆———————

OF WHAT shall a man be proud, if he is not
proud of his friends?

ROBERT LOUIS STEVENSON

———————◆———————

WE INHERIT our relatives and our features
and may not escape them; but we can select
our clothing and our friends, and let us be
careful that both fit us.   VOLNEY STREAMER

THE love of friendship should be gratuitous.
You ought not to have or to love a friend for
what he will give you. If you love him for the
reason that he will supply you with money
or some other temporal favor, you love the
gift rather than him. A friend should be loved
freely for himself, and not for anything else.

ST. AUGUSTINE

THE man that hails you Tom or Jack,
And proves, by thumping on your back,
    His sense of your great merit,
Is such a friend that one had need
Be very much his friend indeed
    To pardon or to bear it.

WILLIAM COWPER

FRIENDSHIP hath the skill and observation of
the best physician, the diligence and vigilance
of the best nurse, and the tenderness and
patience of the best mother.

EDWARD CLARENDON

TAKE envy out of a character and it leaves greater possibilities for friendships.

ELIZABETH B. CUSTER

I HAVE often thought that as longevity is generally desired, and I believe generally expected, it would be wise to be continually adding to the number of our friends, that the loss of some may be supplied by others. Friendship, "the wine of life," should, like a well-stocked cellar, be thus continually renewed; and it is consolatory to think, that although we can seldom add what will equal the generous first-growths, yet friendship becomes insensibly old in much less time than is commonly imagined, and not many years are required to make it very mellow and pleasant. Warmth will, no doubt, make considerable difference.

JAMES BOSWELL

IF A man has a friend, what need has he of medicines?

BHARTRIHARI

THERE is in friendship something of all relations, and something above them all. It is the golden thread that ties the heart of all the world.   JOHN EVELYN

IT IS a wonderful advantage to a man, in every pursuit or avocation, to secure an adviser in a sensible woman. In woman there is at once a subtile delicacy of tact, and a plain soundness of judgment, which are rarely combined to an equal degree in man. A woman, if she be really your friend, will have a sensitive regard for your character, honor, repute. She will seldom counsel you to do a shabby thing; for a woman friend always desires to be proud of you.   SIR EDWARD BULWER-LYTTON

IF WE would build on a sure foundation in friendship, we must love our friends for *their* sakes rather than for *our* own.
                              CHARLOTTE BRONTE

OLD friends are the great blessing of one's latter years. Half a word conveys one's meaning. They have a memory of the same events, and have the same mode of thinking. I have young relations that may grow upon me, for my nature is affectionate, but can they grow old friends?   HORACE WALPOLE

———◆———

THERE are three friendships which are advantageous: friendship with the upright, with the sincere, and with the man of much observation. — Friendship with the man of specious airs, with the insinuatingly soft, and with the glib-tongued, these are injurious.

CONFUCIUS

———◆———

. . . THE communicating of a man's self to his friend worketh two contrary effects, for it redoubleth joys, and cutteth griefs in halfs; for there is no man that imparteth his joys to his friend, but he joyeth the more, and no man that imparteth his griefs to his friend, but he grieveth the less.   FRANCIS BACON

FRIENDSHIP is like a debt of honor; the moment it is talked of, it loses its real name and assumes the more ungrateful form of obligation. From hence we find that those who regularly undertake to cultivate friendship find ingratitude generally repays their efforts.

OLIVER GOLDSMITH

THE years between
Have taught me some sweet,
Some bitter lessons; none
Wiser than this — to
Spend in all things else,
But of old friends,
Be most miserly.

JAMES RUSSELL LOWELL

OINTMENT and perfume rejoice the heart; so doth the sweetness of a man's friend that cometh of hearty counsel. Thine own friend and thy father's friend forsake not.

PROVERBS 27:9

A SWEET word multiplieth friends, and appeaseth enemies, and a gracious tongue in a good man aboundeth.

Be in peace with many, but let one of a thousand be thy counsellor.

If thou wouldst get a friend, try him before thou takest him, and do not credit him easily. . . .

A faithful friend is a strong defense: and he that found him, hath found a treasure. Nothing can be compared to a faithful friend, and no weight of gold and silver is able to countervail the goodness of his fidelity.

ECCLESIASTICUS I:23

CONVEY thy love to thy friend, as an arrow to the mark, to stick there; not as a ball against the wall to rebound back to thee.

FRANCIS QUARLES

FRIENDSHIP is the highest degree of perfection in society.　MICHEL DE MONTAIGNE

ALL men have their frailties; and whoever looks for a friend without imperfections, will never find what he seeks. We love ourselves notwithstanding our faults, and we ought to love our friends in like manner.

CYRUS

He who gets and never gives
Will lose the truest friend that lives;
He who gives and never gets
Will sour his friendships with regrets;
Giving and getting, thus alone
A friendship lives — or dies a-moan!

ALEXANDER MAC LEAN

As you say, we don't need soft skies to make friendship a joy to us. What a heavenly thing it is; "World without end," truly. I grow warm thinking of it, and should glow at the thought if all the glaciers of the Alps were heaped over me! Such friends God has given me in this little life of mine! CELIA THAXTER

THE ornament of a house is the friends who
frequent it.   RALPH WALDO EMERSON

·LITTLE friends may prove great friends.

AESOP

A TRUE friend unbosoms freely, advises just-
ly, assists readily, adventures boldly, takes all
patiently, defends courageously, and con-
tinues a friend unchangeably.

WILLIAM PENN

I WOULD not enter on my list of friends,
 (Tho' graced with polish'd manners and fine
   sense
Yet wanting sensibility) the man
Who needlessly sets foot upon a worm.

WILLIAM COWPER

MY FRIEND is one whom I can associate with
my choicest thoughts.

HENRY DAVID THOREAU

WE TAKE care of our health; we lay up money; we make our roof tight, and our clothing sufficient; but who provides wisely that he shall not be wanting in the best property of all, — friends?

RALPH WALDO EMERSON

A SHALLOW voice said, bitterly, "New
   friend!"
As if the old alone were true, and born
Of sudden freak, the new deserved but scorn
And deep distrust. . . .
. . . The new is older than the old;
And newest friend is oldest friend in this,
That waiting him, we longest grieved to miss
One thing we sought.

HELEN HUNT JACKSON

THERE is a magic in the memory of school-boy friendships; it softens the heart, and even affects the nervous system of those who have no heart.   BENJAMIN DISRAELI

THOU mayest be sure that he that will in private tell thee of thy faults, is thy friend, for he adventures thy dislike, and doth hazard thy hatred; there are few men that can endure it, every man for the most part delighting in self-praise, which is one of the most universal follies that bewitcheth mankind.   SIR WALTER RALEIGH

HE LAUGHED derision when his foes
Against him cast, each man, a stone;
His friend in anger flung a rose —
And all the city heard him moan.
                                ANONYMOUS

BETTER be a nettle in the side of your friend than his echo.   RALPH WALDO EMERSON

THE anxiety of some people to make new friends is so intense that they never have old ones.   ANONYMOUS

Ruɪɴ not yourselves by kindness to others; for that exceeds the due bounds of friendship.

In making friends, consider well first; and when you are fixed, be true, not wavering by reports, nor deserting in affliction, for that becomes not the good and virtuous. Watch against anger; neither speak nor act in it; for like drunkenness, it makes a man a beast, and throws people into desperate inconveniences. Avoid flatterers for they are thieves in disguise; . . . But the virtuous, though poor, love, cherish, and prefer.   Wɪʟʟɪᴀᴍ Pᴇɴɴ
[*Advice to His Children*]

———◆———

Wʜᴇɴ a Friend deals with a Friend, let the bargain be clear and well penn'd,
That they may continue Friends to the End.
                    Bᴇɴᴊᴀᴍɪɴ Fʀᴀɴᴋʟɪɴ

———◆———

Aɴʏʙᴏᴅʏ can sympathize with the sufferings of a friend, but it requires a very fine nature to sympathize with a friend's success.
                    Oꜱᴄᴀʀ Wɪʟᴅᴇ

MY FRIENDS are my estate. Forgive me then
the avarice to hoard them. They tell me those
who were poor early have different views of
gold. I don't know how that is. God is not
so wary as we, else He would give us no
friends, lest we forget Him.

EMILY DICKINSON

A FRIEND whom you have been gaining dur-
ing your whole life, you ought not to be dis-
pleased with in a moment. A stone is many
years becoming a ruby; take care that you do
not destroy it in an instant against another
stone.   SAADI

TURN him and see his threads; look if he be
Friend to himself who would be friend to
 thee.
For that is first requir'd, a man be his own;
But he that's too much that is friend to none.
Then rest, and a friend's value understand,
It is a richer purchase than of land.

BEN JONSON

ARE you playing the same trick again, and trying who can keep silence longest? Remember that all tricks are either knavish or childish; and that it is as foolish to make experiments upon the constancy of a friend as upon the chastity of a wife.

SAMUEL JOHNSON
[*Letter to James Boswell*]

MY FRIEND peers in on me with merry
Wise face, and though the sky stay dim,
The very light of day, the very
Sun's self comes with him.

ALGERNON CHARLES SWINBURNE

NOT chance of birth or place has made us
    friends,
Being oftentimes of different tongues and
    nations,
But the endeavor for the selfsame ends,
With the same hopes, and fears, and
    aspirations.

HENRY WADSWORTH LONGFELLOW

THE tide of friendship does not rise high on the banks of perfection. Amiable weaknesses and shortcomings are the food of love. It is from the roughnesses and imperfect breaks in a man that you are able to lay hold of him. . . . My friends are not perfect — no more than I — and so we suit each other admirably. It is one of the charitable dispensations of Providence that perfection is not essential to friendship.   ALEXANDER SMITH

MY COAT and I live comfortably together. It has assumed all my wrinkles, does not hurt me anywhere, has moulded itself on my deformities, and is complacent to all my movements, and I only feel its presence because it keeps me warm. Old coats and old friends are the same thing.   VICTOR HUGO

I HAVE three chairs in my house: one for solitude, two for friendship, three for company.
                    HENRY DAVID THOREAU

FIRST of all things, for friendship, there must be that delightful, indefinable state called feeling at ease with your companion, — the one man, the one woman out of a multitude who interests you, who meets your thoughts and tastes. JULIA DUHRING

———————◆———————

FRIENDSHIP is only a reciprocal conciliation of interests, and an exchange of good offices; it is a species of commerce out of which self-love always expects to gain something.

FRANÇOIS DE LA ROCHEFOUCAULD

———————◆———————

I WOULDN'T give much for the boy 'at
   grows up
With no friendship subsistin' 'tween him an'
   a pup! EUGENE FIELD

———————◆———————

I DON'T meddle with what my friends believe or reject, any more than I ask whether they are rich or poor. I love *them*.

JAMES RUSSELL LOWELL

WE CANNOT tell the precise moment when friendship is formed. As in filling a vessel drop by drop, there is at last a drop which makes it run over; so in a series of kindnesses there is at last one which makes the heart run over.   JAMES BOSWELL

———————◆———————

Love all, trust a few,
Do wrong to none: be able for thine enemy
Rather in power than use; and keep thy friend
Under thy own life's key.

WILLIAM SHAKESPEARE

———————◆———————

A MAN cannot speak to his son, but as a father; to his wife, but as a husband; to his enemy, but upon terms: whereas a friend may speak, as the case requires, and not as it sorteth with the person.   FRANCIS BACON

———————◆———————

THE more we love our friends, the less we flatter them; it is by excusing nothing that pure love shows itself.

JEAN BAPTISTE MOLIÈRE

HONEST men esteem and value nothing so much in this world as a real friend. Such a one is as it were another self, to whom we impart our most secret thoughts, who partakes of our joy, and comforts us in our affliction; add to this, that his company is an everlasting pleasure to us.   PILPAY

FRIENDSHIP is a vase, which, when it is flawed by heat, or violence, or accident, may as well be broken at once; it can never be trusted after. . . . Coarse stones, if they are fractured, may be cemented again; precious ones never.

WALTER SAVAGE LANDOR

IT IS only the great hearted who can be true friends. The mean and cowardly can never know what true friendship means.

CHARLES KINGSLEY

WHEN friends ask, there is no tomorrow.

PROVERB

MAKE not a bosom friend of a melancholy soul: he'll be sure to aggravate thy adversity, and lessen thy prosperity. He goes always heavy loaded; and thou must bear half. He's never in a good humor; and may easily get into a bad one, and fall out with thee.

THOMAS FULLER

EVERYONE that flatters thee
Is no friend in misery.
Words are easy, like the wind;
Faithful friends are hard to find.
Every man will be thy friend
Whilst thou hast wherewith to spend:
But, if store of crowns be scant,
No man will supply thy want.

RICHARD BARNFIELD

NOTHING is more common than to talk of a friend; nothing more difficult than to find one; nothing more rare than to improve by one as we ought.

ROBERT HALL

WHAT makes us so changeable in our friendships, is our difficulty to discern the qualities of the soul, and the ease with which we detect those of the intellect.

FRANCOIS DE LA ROCHEFOUCAULD

———◆———

O FRIEND, my bosom said,
Through thee alone the sky is arched,
Through thee the rose is red,
All things through thee take nobler form
And look beyond the earth,
And is the mill-round of our fate,
A sun-path in thy worth.
Me too thy nobleness has taught
To master my despair;
The fountains of my hidden life
Are through thy friendship fair.

RALPH WALDO EMERSON

———◆———

FOR not many men, the proverb saith,
Can love a friend whom fortune prospereth
Unenvying.   AESCHYLUS

THE wise man seeks a friend in whom are those qualities which he himself may lack; for thus, being united, is their friendship the more completely defended against adversity.

JEREMY TAYLOR

FLOWERS are lovely; love is flower-like;
Friendship is a sheltering tree;
Oh the joys that came down shower-like,
Of friendship, love, and liberty,
    Ere I was old!

SAMUEL TAYLOR COLERIDGE

THE supreme happiness of life is the conviction of being loved for yourself, or, more correctly, being loved in spite of yourself.

VICTOR HUGO

MY ONLY sketch, profile, of Heaven is a large blue sky, and larger than the biggest I have seen in June — and in it are my friends — every one of them.

EMILY DICKINSON

To be capable of steady friendship and lasting love, are the two greatest proofs, not only of goodness of heart, but of strength of mind.

WILLIAM HAZLITT

We can never replace a friend. When a man is fortunate enough to have several, he finds they are all different. No one has a double in friendship.

JOHANN SCHILLER

If Thought unlock her mysteries
If Friendship on me smile,
I walk in marble galleries,
I talk with kings the while.

RALPH WALDO EMERSON

An elegant sufficiency, content,
Retirement, rural quiet, friendship, books.

JAMES THOMSON

If I mayn't tell you what I feel, what is the use of a friend?

WILLIAM MAKEPEACE THACKERAY

TRUE friendship is of royal lineage. It is of the same kith and breeding as loyalty and self-forgetting devotion and proceeds upon a higher principle even than they. For loyalty may be blind, and friendship must not be; devotion may sacrifice principles of right choice which friendship must guard with an excellent and watchful care. . . . The object of love is to serve, not to win.

WOODROW WILSON

THERE can be no friendship where there is no freedom. Friendship loves a free air, and will not be fenced up in straight and narrow enclosures.
WILLIAM PENN

A FRIENDSHIP will be young after the lapse of half a century; a passion is old at the end of three months.
MADAME SWETCHINE

NEVER contract Friendship with a man who is not better than thyself.
CONFUCIUS

IF A friend of mine . . . gave a feast, and did
not invite me to it, I should not mind a bit. . . .
But if . . . a friend of mine had a sorrow and
refused to allow me to share it, I should feel
it most bitterly. If he shut the doors of the
house of mourning against me, I would move
back again and again and beg to be admitted
so that I might share in what I was entitled
to share. If he thought me unworthy, unfit
to weep with him, I should feel it as the most
poignant humiliation. . . .　　　　OSCAR WILDE

THAT friendship will not continue to the end
which is begun for an end.

FRANCIS QUARLES

TWO PERSONS cannot long be friends if they
cannot forgive each other's little failings.

JEAN DE LA BRUYÈRE

FAR better 'twere for either to be mute,
Than for to murder friendship by dispute.

ROBERT HERRICK

FORSOOTH, brothers, fellowship is heaven, and the lack of fellowship is hell; fellowship is life and the lack of fellowship is death, and the deeds that ye do upon the earth, it is for fellowship's sake that ye do them. Therefore, I bid you not dwell in hell, but in heaven — upon earth, which is a part of heaven and forsooth no foul part.   WILLIAM MORRIS

A FAITHFUL friend is a true image of the Deity.   NAPOLEON BONAPARTE

AFTER friendship it is confidence; before friendship it is judgment.   SENECA

FRIENDSHIP based solely upon gratitude is like a photograph; with time it fades.

CARMEN SYLVA

FRIENDSHIP improves happiness, and abates misery, by doubling our joy, and dividing our grief.   JOSEPH ADDISON

NOTHING more dangerous than a friend without discretion; even a prudent enemy is preferable. JEAN DE LA FONTAINE

NEW friendships are not to be scorned if they offer hope of bearing fruit, like green shoots of corn that do not disappoint us at harvest time. Yet the old friendships must preserve their own place, for the force of age and habit is very great.

... We must be ever on the search for some persons whom we shall love and who will love us in return. If good will and affection are taken away, every joy is taken from life. MARCUS TULLIUS CICERO

PROMISES may get friends, but it is performance that must nurse and keep them.

OWEN FELTHAM

GO OFTEN to the house of thy friend; for weeds soon choke up the unused path.

EDDA [*Scandinavian Mythology*]

THERE are no rules for friendship. It must be left to itself. We cannot force it any more than love. WILLIAM HAZLITT

———◆———

HUMAN friendship has limits because of the real greatness of man. We are too big to be quite comprehended by another. There is always something in us left unexplained, and unexplored. We do not even know ourselves, much less can another hope to probe into the recesses of our being. Friendship has a limit, because of the infinite element in the soul.

HUGH BLACK

———◆———

IT IS delightful to me to go mad over a friend restored to me. HORACE

———◆———

CHOOSE thy friends like thy books, few but choice. JAMES HOWELL

———◆———

NEVER trust a friend who deserts you at a pinch. AESOP

IRON sharpeneth iron; so a man sharpeneth the countenance of his friend.

PROVERBS XXVII: 17

HE WHO is true to one friend thus proves himself worthy of many.   ANONYMOUS

WHO seeks a friend without a fault remains without one.

PROVERB FROM THE TURKISH

I BREATHED a song into the air,
It fell to earth, I knew not where;
For who has sight so keen and strong,
That it can follow the flight of song —

. . . . . .

The song from beginning to end,
I found again in the heart of a friend.

HENRY WADSWORTH LONGFELLOW

THE best preacher is the heart; the best teacher is time; the best book is the world; the best friend is God.   THE TALMUD